Sometimes Two Castles Are Better Than One

By Brittanie Comer

Illustrations by: Tooba Intiaz

This Book Belongs To

____

One day, Aubrey and her mother were walking through the park to Aubrey's father's house.

Aubrey stopped and curiously asked her mother, "Why don't you and Daddy live together anymore?"

Her mother warmly smiled and said, "Let's sit down on the bench so that I can tell you all about it."

Aubrey smiled back and took her mother's outstretched hand. "I would love to hear all about it, Mommy."

"Once upon a time," Aubrey's mother began, "when you were just a baby, your father and I talked about all the fun activities we wanted to do with you as you grew.

On the first day, Mommy began reading the nice books she bought for you, while Daddy practiced playing the drums he purchased for you. Since the drum's music was so loud, Mommy couldn't finish reading."

"It must have been loud!" said Aubrey.
"It sure was!" said her mother, before continuing.

"On the second day, Daddy bought you a small tent to build in the back yard for camping, but Mommy bought you a big pool to teach you how to swim.
MOVING
TENT HOUSE

The pool was so big, Daddy couldn't build the small tent."
TENT HOUSE

"Uh oh!" Aubrey said with her eyes wide. "And then what happened, Mommy?"

"Well," answered her mother, "on the third day, Mommy and Daddy wanted to get you a pet.

Mommy bought you a dog, and Daddy bought you a cat.

But the cat and dog didn't get along very well, so eventually they had to separate the pets by putting them into two different rooms.

"Mommy and Daddy both knew something needed to be done,
so they began to think. And they thought and thought and then
thought some more.

suddenly, they had an idea.

'HOW ABOUT WE BUILD TWO CASTLES!' they said."

"WOW, TWO CASTLES!"
shouted Aubrey.

"Yes, TWO BIG CASTLES!"
said her mother.

"In Mommy's castle, she could read you all the fun books you loved, teach you how to swim in the big pool, and keep the playful pet dog."

In Daddy's castle, he could teach you how to play the loud drums you loved, camp in the small tent in his backyard, and keep the fluffy pet cat.

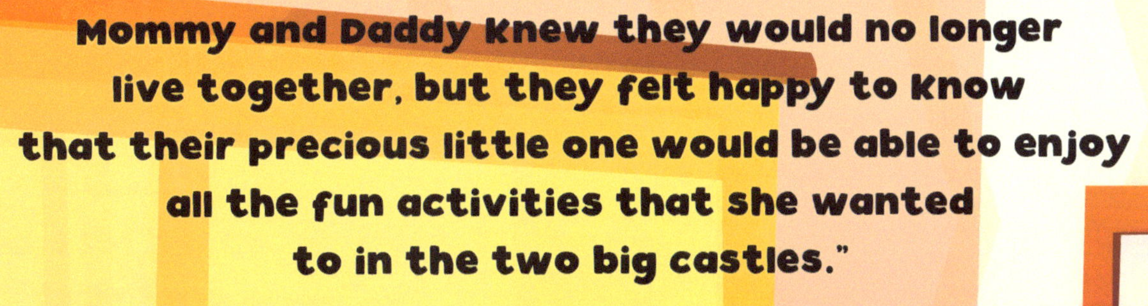
Mommy and Daddy knew they would no longer
live together, but they felt happy to know
that their precious little one would be able to enjoy
all the fun activities that she wanted
to in the two big castles."

Aubrey gazed into her mother's kind eyes and said, "I love my two big castles. And I thank you and Daddy for building them just for me."

Aubrey and her mother stretched their arms out wide and gave each other a big hug. "Sometimes two castles really are better than one," Aubrey said smiling.

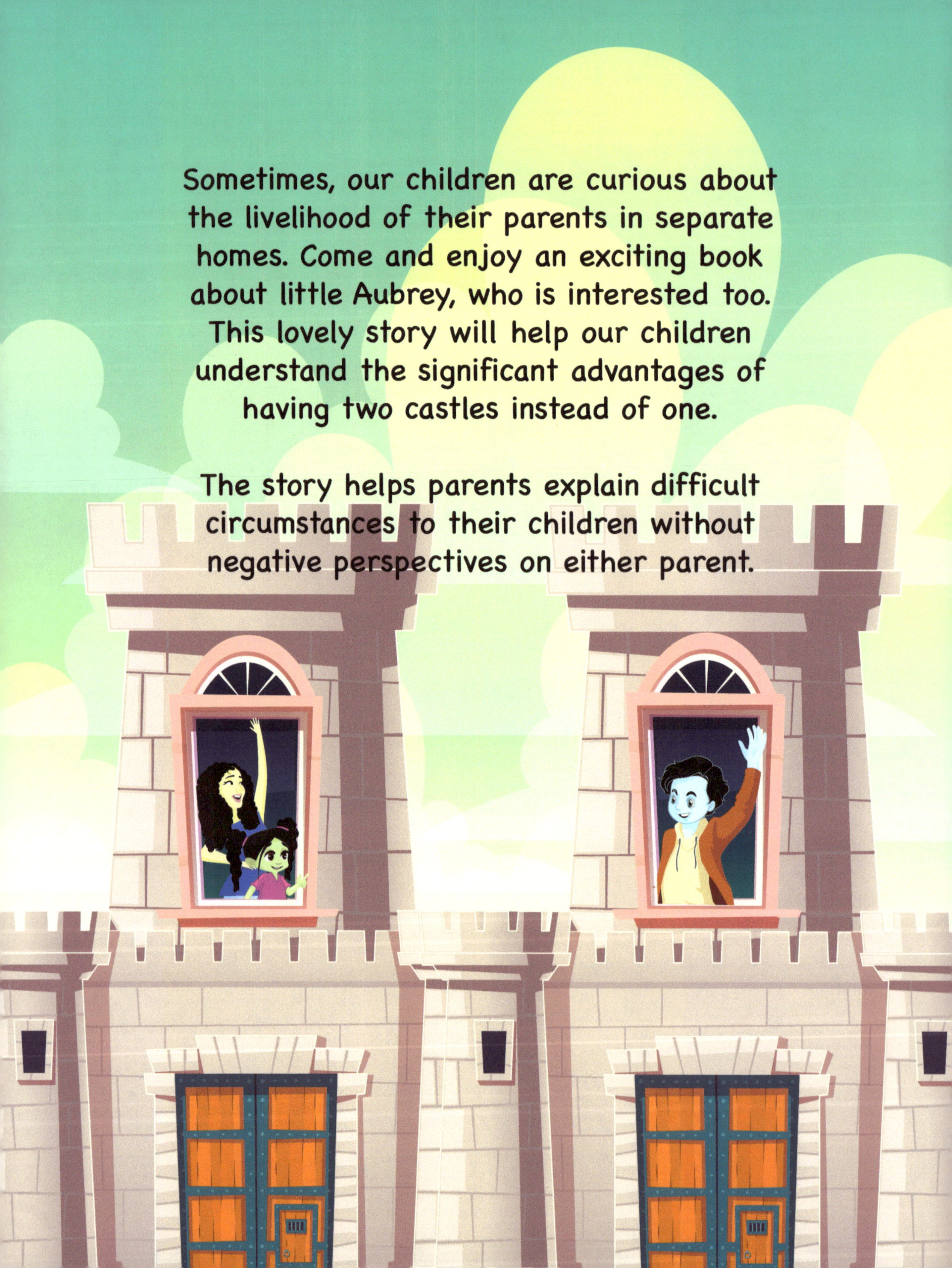

Sometimes, our children are curious about the livelihood of their parents in separate homes. Come and enjoy an exciting book about little Aubrey, who is interested too. This lovely story will help our children understand the significant advantages of having two castles instead of one.

The story helps parents explain difficult circumstances to their children without negative perspectives on either parent.